WANTING

WRITTEN BY RALPH WATKINS

POETRY AND PROSE

FIRST AMERICAN BOOK IN PRINT

WWW.DCNATIVESON.COM
PUBLISHER: AUDAX PUBLISHING SERVICES, LLC.
ALL COPYRIGHTS RESERVED COPYRIGHT 2014
EMAIL: DMVPOET@GMAIL.COM
PUBLISHED DISTRICT HEIGHTS, M.D.
PRINT IN AMERICA SEPTEMBER 2019

PREFACE

WANTING IS A BOOK OF POETRY AND PROSE BY RALPH WATKINS JR., DESIGNED FOR FAMILY, FRIENDS, AND PEOPLE OF VARIOUS CULTURES AND OF MATURE AGE; THAT LOVE READING MODERN, AND URBAN LITERARY CREATIVE WORK. THROUGH THESE PAGES YOU ARE ABLE TO FEEL MY HEARTBEAT, READ MY THOUGHTS AND RUMMAGE THROUGH MY BAGGAGE OF LIFE CHOICES. OFTEN REFLECTING ON INCIDENTS OF PAST ACTIONS, FAMILY, AND RELATIONSHIPS EXPERIENCES OF A SPIRITUAL OR SECULAR NATURE, COPYRIGHT RAW MATERIAL IN TEXT.

THE BODY OF WORK STRETCHES OVER 40 YEARS, FROM EARLY CHILDHOOD, AND MILITARY EXPERIENCES, WHICH ENCOMPASSES AND DEPICTS VARIOUS LIFE, FAMILY, AND SOME FAMILIAR EXPERIENCES INVOLVING RELATIONSHIP WITH PEOPLE. POETRY HAS ALWAYS BEEN A USEFUL TOOL TO SHARE, ENCOURAGE OTHER PEOPLE.

ONE OF MY BIGGEST DREAMS, GOES AS FAR BACK AS I CAN REMEMBER, AND THAT IS TO BE A CREATIVE WRITER OF POETRY AND SHORT STORIES. I DID NOT TAKE A DIRECT PATH, AND I WAS NOT ALWAYS FOCUSED. BUT MY HEART WAS ALWAYS IN THE RIGHT PLACE. IN MY HEART, I KEPT THIS LOVE FOR WRITING POETRY ALIVE. OVER THE YEARS I WOULD REVISIT THE THOUGHT OF WRITING A COMPLETE BOOK OF POETRY. I HAVE ARRIVED AT A PLACE, WHEREAS I CAN NO LONGER WAIT OR PUT OFF MY DREAM, UNTIL TOMORROW.

Content

- I Am Innocent — 10
- The Best Day — 11
- Storms — 12
- I Don't Want You — 13
- Hit or Miss — 14
- Still — 15
- Thanks Day — 16
- Missing You — 17
- Hurt — 18
- Lord I Know — 19
- Mental Institution — 20-21
- Fear — 22
- Black Family Reunion — 23
- Yo Yo — 24-25
- In Plain Sight — 26-27
- Don't Say A Word — 28-29
- I Do Pray — 30
- Holding My Heart — 31
- Mistaken — 32
- A Mother's Love — 33
- Air Breathe — 34-35
- Lover's Quarrel — 36
- Soft Ground — 36-37

- Why Before Now — 38
- Got To Have It — 39
- Photograph — 40
- I Want So Badly — 41
- Change — 42
- Why Do I — 43
- I Love You — 44
- Three Chances — 45
- I Keep Trying — 46
- I Was — 47
- I Remember When — 48-49
- You Got Me — 50-51
- One Day — 52-53
- Even Though — 54-55
- Lost My Pen — 56-57
- Sometimes — 58-59
- No Good — 60-61
- Never — 62
- My Grandmother — 63

- No More — 64
- Acting A Fool — 65
- Black History — 66
- It's Not My Fault — 67
- Runner's Creed — 68
- I Did Not Have To — 69
- The "N" Word — 70
- A Race Against The Old Me — 71
- My Child — 72
- Unleashed — 73
- I Need You — 74
- You Can't — 75
- Mr. Window — 76
- Disappointed — 77
- The Little People — 78
- No One Touches My Heart — 79
- Me Oh My — 80
- It's All About Me — 81

♦	Boogie	82
♦	I'm In A Struggle	83
♦	My Drunken Heart	84-85
♦	No Matter What It Looks Like	86-87
♦	Have You Been Faithful?	88
♦	Saying Goodbye	89
♦	Frank "The Barber"	90-91
♦	Let Me Break This Down	92-93
♦	The Greatest Gift Is Love	94
♦	Real Friends	95
♦	My Parents Were Right	96-97

I Am Innocent

I didn't do it,
no matter what it
looks like.
I know my hands
were caught in the
cookie jar.
And the fact that I
have cookie crumbs
all over my face.
I want to state for the
record that it wasn't me, and
I didn't do it.
Just let me know if
I am going need a Lawyer;
there's no way I am
defending myself.
*(Dam right, I am a flight
risk but only I know that).*
It's bad enough that they have
me on house arrest, with
this ankle bracelet.
What had happened was,
I stuck my hand in the cookie jar,
and I then had a change of heart.
At that moment, I became
overwhelmed and remorseful
with tears, and started wiping
my face. That's when the
Store Owner walked in. I rest my case.

The Best Day

I am going to get up,
and try to make this
the best day of my life.
It's not my birthday,
it's not a holiday and
I have to go to work
like everyone else.
I realize it's time
for some changes
in my life, and they're
not going to happen
by themselves.
Something inside of me
has to be more positive
than its ever been before.
Maybe, I'll see an opportunity
to open another closed door.

Storms

All we have left are the remaining broken pieces. We can try to put them back together, knowing what we have will never be the same as what we had.

Let's not kid ourselves about that, let us find a broom and a dust pan, and sweep it up and throw it all away and start over.

There's a lot to be said about storms. Storm comes in everyone's life, and we still could have lost everything, a lot more than hurt feelings. Those can get better over time if you give them a chance and time to heal.

I Don't Want You

I don't want you
To start crying now
When you see me
With someone else.
You were never there
When I needed you.
Not even in my mind,
When you were right
By my side, and holding
My hand.

I wanted you to know,
I needed to mean more
To you than somebody that
Keeps you warm at night,
And that smiles every time for
The camera for everyone else to see.

I'm almost sure baby,
You will find someone else
To fill the void, but no one
With the love, I had in my heart for you.

One day you'll wake up,
And see the love you've lost,
Is currently with someone else.
Baby, it will be all your fault,
Because no one holds onto
A love, that doesn't love them
Back, nobody.

Hit or Miss

In this relationship you can say one thing and mean something else. Which means you're being unfair and thoughtless towards the other person.

Don't tell me, you think you know me better than I know myself as a legitimate excuse. You are still reasonably obligated not to try and hurt my feelings in the process. I am not perfect, even as I get older.

I realize I am making more mistakes, but the beauty of my expectations is that you are here to help me, and not to hurt me. Let the choice of choosing you, be of no consequence to me now.

So, morning came and went without repairs to our relationship. A ship can only take on so many tears before it sinks. And it looks like we're on uncharted waters. The biggest problem with relationships are that most people want to abandon ship, instead of working out the problem.

Still

She still never looked back,
I just want to vent,
is that ok?
I don't want to
reinvent the wheel.
Somethings are for me.
Somethings are for
someone else.
I just want to know
when you're with me,
how did I make you feel?
I don't want to go through
the motions, if we
can't be real with one another.
I would rather be by
myself, amuse myself
or pretend that
I am the man of steel.
I want to be happy, or
by myself, that's for real.

Thanks Dad

Thank you dad, for sharing the best you had. Everybody has a heaven that they can't touch, and it's a place waiting for them at the end of their road.

When they've done all they can and suppose to do; God is calling them home.

I heard my dad say this a million times, "One day son I am going to have to leave this world behind. Please, when it happens, don't let it come as a big surprise. We all have to go at some time or another.

Just learn to live your life the best way you can. Treat folks right, with respect and believe in a God that you can see, if you seek Him out. And, when you get to heaven, you'll be sitting, between Him and me, and that's the place you want to be."

Missing You

And I never thought
love like yours
couldn't be replaced
every time I look
in the mirror.

I can see "missing you."
All on my face.
I sit up at night
because it doesn't
seem right,
that you and I
are not together
tonight.

Hurt

What's it's going to hurt
for me to walk away?
What's it's going to hurt
to stop calling you,
when I know you
love someone else?
What's it's going to hurt
to let you go on, with
you knowing I am
standing on your front porch
with puppy dog eyes,
hoping you'd come back to me?
It's going to hurt me
but I want to see you happy,
even if it's not with me.
As sad as a statement a person
can come to realize,
"If I only knew then, what
I know now."

Lord I Know

Lord I know, it was one of your angels flying too close to the ground.
I remember, the first day I saw her.
She was my angel sent from heaven.

I knew then everything had to be perfect. My attitude was to go slow, and don't stumble but make a good impression.

I was in the early days of my youth, and the feeling back then was nothing but the truth. The tender years went by.

And, so much of our body mechanism changes; one or two chance encounter, but nothing like when I first saw them, none the less the angel I first saw. No matter the distance or differences between us now, I still love and miss you.

Mental Institution

One day, I just woke up feeling a lot of pain, and it never went away, like an uninvited relative, after speaking with my doctor, it's here to stay.

You laugh at first, thinking of all the fun days in the past, then you start to think these relatives after asking nicely, begging, and pleading to God, they are still not going to leave.

I have come to the same conclusion as you have; I must be under the influence, and these people are not my relatives, they are institutional boarded and fed meds every day like I am.

Oh my soul, my God to be if you can hear me, come to rescue me. I am wearing a white cotton T-shirt and white skive undershorts.

Not so funny now, how I use to laugh, and pass judgment or seemingly ignore those that had more mental and physical issues then I did. But look who's crying now?

Mister, I've got the world by the balls, picture-perfect house, family, and health. Now, I am dialing 1-800- 911-Jesus please save me.

It's never too late to call on the Lord; just know how long you've kept Him waiting on you or on hold. Sunday service, Wednesday bible study, and last but certainly not least, accepting Him as your personal Lord. As you've figured out by now, Savior.

Fear

Be like a baby for its first time without reservation, hesitation or expectations. They come running and screaming out of its mother's womb dressed for battle. And without damaging their little heart or spirit, you have to encourage them to run as fast as they can, jump knowing no limits, and agree with them when they say, "Look, mommy and daddy, I can fly. Yes, baby, you can fly because you and I never learned to fly.

But at the same time, we need to stop leaving conflicts and wars for our children to finish or try to settle. Because we're afraid to find resolution through peaceful means, without guns and nuclear threats.

If we're not very careful, we won't have a world left, and no one to blame but ourselves. This, my friend is what I fear the most?

Our children are our green Berets, born into a world of conflicts and wars, and the last thing they need to know or feel is fear. Yes, we do realize when it's time to come home.

Especially, when there's no more fight left in us. I can't run as fast, I can't jump without further damaging myself. "I am sorry mom and dad, I never learn to fly." And let us leave no more than we have to on the plates of our children, and this Nation.

Black Family Reunion

Nothing like an all Black family reunion. You see people you have not seen in a very long time_ You kiss and hug, but hard to embrace for the sad occasion.

We all know that one day we're all going to pass away, but what we don't know is the for certain order that we have to say good bye. It's these black and sad occasions that we come together to send off a heavenly angel.

Their time on earth has come for some, has come too soon. But here we all are celebrating the life and relationship we had, and the fond memories they left behind.

Its also then, some of us feel "some kind of way" because their relationship with the deceased was strand or estrange.

Fortunately, with God, we make peace and move forward in our lives. Truly this person that has touched our lives will be truly missed, and we will see them again if it be God's will. But I pray, and we should all pray with me, "Lord, take this angel back into your arms."

Yo Yo

Let me talk to you for a minute. I can tell you're
not from around here. Why don't you wise up
or go the hell back home. You look so out of place,
you're not blending in with your own race.
Get whatever you're looking for and leave. You got
a lot of leaves moving around here, when there's
no breeze.

I know it's still early and you might have enough
time to make up your mind. Take the 1 o'clock
Greyhound, and get out of town. Sometimes
in life or in a relationship, we don't see the poten-
tial or our own demise.

If we don't stop and listen to our conscience or
trust our gut feeling, we're only going to see our-
selves laying in a back alley victimized, or dead for
sure as we ascend up, with our heavenly suit on.

Yo yo
If you don't listen to me, go ahead and take your chances. Life is not about being a hero. It's about being smart and knowing when to get out of some place you don't belong.

Yeah, you can take your chances and you might survive, if that's a chance you're willing to take. Again, if you're not hooked on God here on earth with his angels watching your back, you could be making deals with the devil that you don't know about. Sometimes in life, you have to wake up to what is really happening around you.

IN PLAIN SIGHT

In plain sight, laying back in the cut, camouflaged by my surroundings, and blending in. I see things all the time, without prejudice or being hypocritical, and without other people knowing.

I'm there and watching. I saw who robbed who, when they weren't home. I saw who was cheating on who, when they thought
They were alone.

Tell you the truth. I need help, trying not to close my eyes or look the other way. But trust me, i will tell on myself before I tell on any of you. I know the God I serve is forever watching over me.

I can also tell you, the government is corrupt, just ask Edward Snowden that.
Don't ever trust what you're drinking from an open cup, and it's sad to know, that
Even the self-righteous can't get it right.

I just happened to be minding my own business and couldn't help to notice, the things people do when they think the world is asleep, at work or damn it, not looking.

Of course, if you ask them, they're going to deny it. Even if you come home early and catch them in that lie. People will go to their grave having you believe the picture they've painted for you, than to simply tell you the truth.

DON'T SAY A WORD

This is a City within a City. There are places within this City you shouldn't go. And there are people inside this City that I hope you never meet or get to know. Three things people fail to realize in life, you can't run fast enough, you can't hide deep enough, and you should never borrow money, you don't know who the lenders are.

These guys lend money to people down on their luck, then they sit around and bet 100-1, you don't pay it all back. They don't have a fixed interest or flex spending plan when you've earnestly come back to pay them; this is the part you don't understand. We don't want the money back, we want your life. We want you to work for us, and we, in turn, will let you live. Now, you're standing there wondering what in the hell have you gotten yourself into?

I've always known about the dark side of Washington, D.C. but I've always known to avoid certain places, people and never borrow money when I don't know who the lenders are. Because these guys play for keeps, and there's no paying them back.

They prey on the weak, drug users, gamblers, school children, Doctors, Lawyers, and Home Owners. Get the picture. No one is exempt. Once you get involved, who are you going to tell? You'll just become another unidentified body somewhere and another unlucky poor son of a bitch to them.

I work for these people. I look for people, and I help bring them back. I get phone calls with names of people on the run or in hiding. My only job is to inquire about their whereabouts and dime them out.

I myself got caught up and recruited years ago. I tried to run, couldn't run. I tried to hide but found myself in a worse predicament, and just when I thought it was safe to do so, I went and reported my doings and theirs to the Police. They looked at me, and said, "No more warnings buddy, we're on the same team." Unbeknownst to me, my nephew is in town, I would have never known immediately if his name didn't appear on my list to find.

So, this is the beginning of the story. Looking to save my nephew. By the time I run into others like myself in this City, that are out here reporting, says, "your nephew is in deep for $200,000. And, he's running and the odds on the street he'll be dead by tomorrow, not worth the Lenders time or money."

I Do Pray

I did ask God, "What am I doing
wrong?" I do pray, and I ask God to
show me the errors of my ways.
To have had the love I've lost,
it's cause to summon all my angels
to pray with me.

To let them know,
we cannot afford
to let something like this
to ever happen again,
tough lesson to learn
at a very high cost.

Looking back, I should
have been more caring,
and gentle, especially
when it came to matters
of the heart.

So, here I sit
with both hands clasp
together praying, that
God gives me another
chance, knowing He's
already giving me many
Before this request.

Holding My Heart

Who is this Lover holding my heart, and crying at the same time? Has their love become too toxic for me to breathe? I am in this dream, I am not alone. Ask yourselves the same question, who is this person? I can't save myself in this dream.

The sound of my own heart pounding would make a few of us stop to think, what have I done wrong? Dirt is pouring in from everywhere. The sight of me fighting back as I try to push dirt up off of me. More and more, as I started to understand what was going on.

You just can't love someone for real or pretentiously, and move on with your life because you feel like it. There are emotional and spiritual ties that still exist in the heart of the mind, of the other person. Looking back, every debt can't be settled with gold.

Spooky, as it may sound, they hold a dead man's fate in their hands. There have been more casualties in love than in war. I woke up with this message: know who and what you're dealing with, pray and make amends. The thoughts of others we leave behind could make for a very happy funeral of our own doing. Once dead, but twice buried.

Mistaken

I am not of this world, I was born into it too soon or too late. I was born and raised with good moral fibers, over the years the, "Thee I sing," and the flag I believe in has done nothing but wither.

I am all for Civil and Equal Rights Under the Law, but people, we have to draw a line in the sand somewhere. Just because Mike and Sam, Tina and Pat love one another, doesn't entitle them to marry each other. If, you've somehow made it into this country illegal, know this, you are trespassing and are in violation of our laws and statutes, and I am not mad at you either.

We make too many excuses, we either are or we aren't going to do something about domestic violence. We are failing to stand up on sound doctrine, Constitutional Rights that are impenetrable. No, I am not saying all our Forefathers were right, but they had a good idea.

Nothing has changed, seemingly. It's still modern day slavery of our minds. The overseers don't need whips or chains, we are doing it to ourselves. When they took the pledge of allegiance out of public schools, I thought I was done then, same sex marriages and followed by legalized marijuana was put into law in several states; the moral majority has lost its mind.

I don't dislike people, individually or as a whole. I see a much bigger picture. If we don't provide better laws, that will protect people from living immoral lives and patriotic allegiance to our government on its foundation, we're going to need more than band aides and bullets to fix it.

A Mother's Love

There's no way I could have done this
without you in my life.
You've made every mountain
I've ever climbed seem low.

You held me up in the beginning,
and said, "Just keep walking."
From there, I never looked back.
I know you've always had my back,
and you would catch me if I fell.

Nothing but encouraging words,
and necessary taps on my butt and hands.
But while looking up at your face, it always
seemed to hurt you way more than me.

I love you mother more than
spoken or printed words in a Hallmark card.
As I look back, I see you're still there,
with caring arms extended wide open,
gentle smile and that light of hope for me in
your eyes.

And prayers from your hearts,
that can be seen from your eyes.
I never stop trying to better myself
Because of you and you alone. You've
made all the difference in my life.
Thank you mother, for always being there
for me.

Air Breathe

Water tease
Wind breeze
Rain pain
Sun run
Dry climate
Height freighted
Valley low
Mountain climb
Falling fast
Accident crash
Wounded veteran
Bomb explodes
Crazy drug
Paranoia stress
Final destination
Unfortunate death
Love pain
Again begin
Tireless life Home.

My humble beginnings you helped mold me. So much unconditional love and attention. Where would I be without you? No matter where I am, you're forever on my mind or in my heart.

On those days, I am feeling down and need to find that inner strength, it's those encouraging words from friends and neighbors, "Always remember where you come from." Home, no other place like it in the world.

Lover's Quarrel

For all my Lovers' quarrels unsettled and still on the table. I still have you on my mind, as I turn these curves and make my way up these hills. Just be happy for me right now, as I am for all of you. You don't know how many other people are experiencing some of the same kinds things you're going through, as a husband, wife, parents, or with medical issues, mental episodes, and disorders.

You are not alone, yet most of us suffer alone or die slowly each day by not dealing with the problem or facing the issue, and ignoring the obvious. But, if you just open your mouth and share what's going on with you, that's keeping you from smiling, someone just might be able to help you or share a similar situation, on how they got through it.

Many times, when I wasn't sure about something, and I elected to weigh out the hurt and pain. That later became much too late. Until, I am just sitting up in a hospital, wondering how I got here or in my closet refusing to come out.

Life does become over-burdensome sometimes. It's then, we have to realize, we need a break or say to someone, "I think I need help." Or, "I am hurting from the inside." I know a lot of tall and strong people, but behind closed doors and accompanied with pride, which always seems to come before the fall. Look in the mirror and say to self, "We need help before it's too late."

Soft Grounds

I am a Soldier. My father was a Soldier, and his father was a blessed Soldier of the cloth, and so forth. The red blood bled for freedom, for their children and their children's children. It's our call to serve and duty, with the slightest wind change.

My father would say, "Don't start a fight, don't wage war and always pick and choose your own battles. And, if you're coming to the aide of a friend or brother, just help them and get the hell out of there."

Every day, we're at war, foreign or domestic. It doesn't mean it's not happening, because you don't see or hear any bullets flying or missiles coming over our heads.

Peace is that thing we work hard towards and look diligently for but know that it does not exist in every Soldier's heart or mind. We pray that others find it, and it's a small token from us to them, from wars past and rumored. Just enjoy it, sleep well and pray that peace remains with us.

Way Before Now

I needed you way before now, yesterday was way too late. I walked you home every day after school until our blue skies turned to grey. We both knew we had to refrain from embracing and go our separate ways. Then, I met someone else that made me smile as much as you did. We laughed and played so much, it drowned out the fun we had.

Then, I heard the sound of the marching band playing, and someone yelling out, "Marine," you have to join in. I had to refrain from embracing those grey skies, that pushed all the blue skies away.
With my past behind me, I took another chance at romance. Several times over, I went knocking and had to pay, but I always walked away with a smile on my face.

Then one day I woke up and I prayed, "God send me someone special who will love me, and never go away." I am a believer, and He answered my prayers. We married, and had children, moved around until we settled down." But, the story doesn't end here.

Got To Have It

It's 3 a.m., and I have yet to get my freak on. She was up struggling to help me but fell asleep in the process. It's nobody's fault, it doesn't look like I am going to be able to pull this off. It looks like my, "Get up and go," has got up and gone. The train never came into the station. I was trying by saying, " I know I can, I know I can!"

Then I looked at her and said, "are you up for a game of scrabble?" Needless to say, she could spell her ass off. It didn't help make my situation any better. I said, "so what do you charge your customers when they have this kind of problem." She said, "I usually charge them double because sitting up at three O'clock in the morning, playing with someone's you know what, and a game of scrabble is not part of the deal."

"And if I wanted to play scrabble, I could have stayed home with my husband and kids." I picked up my chin and closed my mouth. I told her to just take an extra $100 from my wallet. I went to bed and laid flat on my stomach. I am thinking, I need to take up crocheting or something. I feel like my screwing days are numbered. This is not how I thought my night would have ended.

PHOTOGRAPH

Every man she ever knew treated her wrong, always made her feel unwanted and unworthy at the same time. Her father took advantage of her in ways, a child should never know.

Her husband abused her with words, and with the palm of his hands to both sides of her face. He convinced her, you'll never find another man like me. To feed you, clothe you and keep a roof over your head.

There were many nights, she had wished she was never born, or that she was dead. Episodes later, she gave birth to a son. Promised herself, that he'll never be like her father or his dad. Damn, this curse has got to stop. She prayed daily, took him to church each Sunday, and anointed him with oil from head to toe.

As he got older, he bucked once at her and she knocked him clear to the floor. "Before you get up son, if you ever try me again, think or have any other thoughts of trying me. I will introduce you to God myself. I am more than worthy, and I want nothing more than this devil to go away."

I WANTED SO BADLY

I wanted so badly for this thing to work out, between you and I. I was ready, willing and able to repair the bridge that had fallen down between us.

But you kept walking away, leaving me to contend with the demons that separated us from the beginning. I tried my best to spend more time with you, but you always left me wondering what's going on with you?

So, I found myself looking for someone else to love and give me some special attention. But, when you finally came around, there was nothing I failed to mention.

Sadly, no one can live like this, not knowing from one day to the next, which way the other person is going. But, I know I can't do this not knowing someone else's heart. Especially, if they don't tell you.

CHANGE

I know everyone changes but what changed your mind? You use to give me so much attention, now you don't pay me any mind. I never did anything to you. I can see your attitude and demeanor has changed. We use to hold small conversations, now you just up and walk away.

All I ever did was pour you a cup of coffee, ask you," Does this complete your order?" You'd look up at me, and say," Have a real nice day." Now, you don't even come to my side of the counter.

I want to know what's the matter? Before I can say, hello, you were already walking out the door. And you won't let me wait on you anymore. I never ask you for anything. No cash, diamond or the promise of anything. All I know is you won't even look at my way.

What changed you? From you allowing me to serve you, the things you want each day, and with a smile? Somewhere along the way, someone else must have treated you wrong, and now you want to blame the world. Every now and then, we meet up with people and they don't treat us right. But we can't take that bad experience from one person to the next.

You were my customer, and I would like to see you smile again. I don't know what changed you, or who changed your heart. And in this unique situation, the customer is not right. Because you never gave me a chance to keep what we have.

Why Do I

Why do I keep letting this thing, keep beating me up? They are not coming back home. I can stop looking out the window. They're long gone and moved on with their lives. It's just that, I've never had a defeated attitude or mentality. But, that may not correlate with the real world or my current situation.

When I said that I love you, I didn't think that one day with all my efforts and good intent, that you would leave. I am glad no one can see me right now.

My tears are rolling down my face like rain against a window pane. I wanted so much for that relationship to work, but it didn't stand a chance when I found myself operating the ship alone.

Now, I am caught up in my own storm. I got myself in it. And now, I have to chart a healthy course out of it. I didn't abandon the ship. I didn't jump ship. But, I am not about to go down with the ship, when I am the only one left on board.

I Love You

I stood there and here, and over there. For countless days thinking of countless ways. And it did not matter the time of season or the weather, but I had a reason. I tried to find the right words and I tried to listen to the little bird, and still, there was something not added or missing.

So, I wrote down these words and it took everything I knew about myself and life to describe how I feel. It bought me to tears, and to my knees, *that I didn't want to live without you or go another step without you.* Because I want to hear babies crying and laughing, as I lay down beside you, contemplating our lives together.

Imagine what it would be like if we were really together. But that is too far fast forward. Let me share with you where I am right now. I just want to say, what I couldn't say in a way that I couldn't understand until now, I love you.

THREE CHANCES

When she called me last night, I should have read her the words from the last sympathy card, that she had sent me. But, I was in a forgiving mood, so I told her don't pack anything and come on over. She showed up with a smile and tears in her eyes. She jumped right up on my lap, exclaiming how much she had missed me, and it had been awhile. I didn't say much in response, just sat there and closed my eyes.

She asked me, "What do I want to do?" I told her, "Tonight I want to play hard to get." She asked me, "What do you mean by that?" I said, "I had a long day, I really don't feel like being bothered, and I would prefer that you sleep out here on the couch." She looked at me, and said, "You don't play fair." I realize every time we get together, you end up leaving me for someone else. And I end up sitting out here with my feelings and face in my hands.

We don't have a relationship, and I don't feel like filling in for someone else. Good night, and please be gone by three 3 a.m., or make up your mind that you're going to stay. Then one day, you just might get me. And we won't have to play these games anymore. Sorry, Charlie, tricks don't work in my neighborhood.

I KEEP TRYING

I keep trying
to pick up the broken pieces,
it's just so many
and they're all
over the place.
And, if I pick them up,
do I try to put
them together?
Or do I sweep them up
in my dustpan and
throw them all away?
I know, I have to start from
somewhere. Where is
my beginning, if I still
have yesterday's broken
pieces of relationship all
over the place?
I need time to figure this out,
about who goes, and who stays;
and why should I feel sorry?
I didn't act alone.
Folks get to pushing all my wrong buttons,
and they find out that's not how I get down.
And it's at that time, for them to roll.
I am sweeping these broken pieces,
out the front door.

I WAS HAPPY

I was happy
at one point,
at some point
Now it points
at some point,
I am hoping
things will change.
And no point
explaining how
at some point
things just changed.
At one point
you were always there.
At some point
you would just disappear.
At this point
I don't care.
At some point
you will come back,
and I won't be here.
I hope you get the point,
at some point but my point is,
why am I still here?

I Remember When

I was ordinary, I didn't cause any problems
or give any worries.

One day I woke up and got tired of being worked over like a $2 hoe or being beaten' up like one.

I had to do something different, like change my ways, stop the revolving door and people from entering into my life with no good intentions. And get rid of the ones, that don't seem to go away.

So, I gave myself some rules to live by, and I had my dear sweet grandmother give me some good advice, as she made me a not for Halloween costume, I can be Superman!

I remember wiping my tears, and saying,
"You don't have to get out but you have got to leave!

Stop calling.
Stop texting messages.
Stop visiting me, this is not the Holiday Inn.
And stop thinking I am going to change my mind, ever again.

And no! We can't just be friends.
That stuff don't work, because I find myself, two or three months later down the road looking or feeling like a found on the side of the road teddy bear.

The time has come for old things to past away, and make a way for a new beginning.
As my grandmother would say, "This is going to hurt me, more than it's going hurt you." But, in the long run, I will be better than okay.

You Got Me

I don't know how to love,
it hurts every time I try.
Every time I get myself in
too deep, I start to cry.

It always seems like unfamiliar
territory, I don't know what to do
or what to say.
I find myself when the other
person is not looking, just walking away.

I have been hurt before, but when
morning came, I found myself sitting on the
edge of the bed like a stuffed teddy bear,
waiting for them to come back home.

I waited way too long before I realized,
I needed to get up and move on with my life.
Many would say I needed to grow up,
those kinds of things happen, its a part
of life.

But what they don't seem to understand, it's that part of my heart, I can never get back. I am trying to be a big boy, but I see I am going to need a little more time, a lot more time.

I don't think she knows when she stole my heart, she took the part of me I can never give to anyone else. Yes, I am having another moment.

Relationships are turning into revolving doors. Just keep it moving baby! I don't know who to feel sorrier for anymore, me or them. My true blue feelings are that she returns, putting my heart back where it belongs.

ONE DAY

I lost my mind, and
when I regain my senses,
everyone that could breathe
left out running and the rest
were left breathless, or not stand-
ing. I am wondering,
why didn't anyone
try to stop me?
or come to save me.
I stayed there
on the stage
and touched the Mic
to see if it was still on.
And I live another day
with no opportunity,
but it's not just my struggle alone,
as I struggle alone, for this just
cause for solidarity and unity.
Now, who alone, wants to pick up
the mic and be with me?
For one moment
you allowed
this broken-hearted Poet
to speak his mind.
I gave them hell as
I brought down heaven,
as I rested the Mic down
when I finished.
It was a moment

I was inspired,
but I can't remember.
Why didn't someone
stop me?
Who gave
this rock to me?
I knew
I should have
stayed at home,
prayed at home.
Now, mothers
are out there
looking for their
sons and daughters.
Never let a Poet
out of your sight,
they just might
pick up the Mic.
Condemn the whole
damn building,
and say to the Head Contractor
"Let's rebuild, and change
the site."
I want peace and harmony
within my soul and outside,
as I look out my window,
not just for myself but for every-
one.

EVEN THOUGH

Even though we've both
moved on
with someone new,
I still can't
get these thoughts
of you
out my head,
and I don't know
what to do.
Why didn't it
work out?
I was such
a jerk
back then.
And, I never thought
love like yours
couldn't be replaced.
Every time I look
in the mirror,
I can still see missing you
all in my face.
I sit up at night,
because it doesn't
seem right,
that you and I
are not together
tonight.

I have to find
a way to get over you,
and make the one
that I have next to me feel
brand new,
before I lose her,
like I lost you.
By not paying them any attention.
Was there anything
I left out, or failed to mention?

Lost My Pen

For those that don't know,
I lost my pen
the other day.
I saw it rollaway
as my hands were
being locked behind
my back in cuffs.
I did turn for a second, as
I tried to resist.
I told them that you are trying
to hurt me.
I couldn't write.
I couldn't call.
I couldn't do anything
except wait to plead
my case.
Of course, she held
me in contempt,
because I spoke out of turn
and I spoke my mind.
I said, "You don't play fair
and you won't let me explain
myself."

So, now I write to you, don't get yourself into a situation, that you and bail money won't be able to get you out of the same night.

I am having this pointless conversation, with this very interesting person, she's telling me in so many words or less, that she's in a relationship. I am diplomatically telling her in so many words or less.

I don't care, who makes you breakfast in the morning, father of your two children or who rubs your feet at night. I just want to know, do you have space for one more in your taxi cab, because I am a paying customer?

SOMETIMES

Sometimes, the body and mind
are just too tired to play games,
this is one of those days.
I am not going to go outside.

I am not going to answer the
the telephone. I don't feel
like having to explain myself
to anyone about how I feel.
I know that I don't have any
wind blowing in my sails.
Anything I attempt to do today,
it would only fail.

Y'all will just have to go on
without me, I concede.
Go ahead, and play your games,
without me today.

I try to avoid these little situations of getting involved with other people, who are already involved with other people or these types of situations, however, they may appear.

They have all the potential of getting me hurt. It's hard to fight back when you know you're wrong. And until or unless that situation changes without your assistance or involvement, stay as far away as you possibly can. You don't see it at first, but you will be the one eventually hurt, and not just sometimes.

No Good

Oh, baby,
in my bedroom voice,
make me your first choice.
I won't neglect any of
your needs.
I will flirt first
make you dessert first.
You can take off
my shirt first.
Oh, baby,
don't act like you don't know.
I want to tie you down
to my bedpost,
and not let you go.
Drip hot wax down
your spine, take
you on a journey
and do things that
you won't be able
to tell your momma'.

Your dependency, but I knew I wasn't
your supplier, once you got away from
me. You were weak and was making me
even weaker. And I know the God, and
where I come from. Doing drugs is dumb.
I love you, but not the drugs inside of
you or the things that you do.

Be afraid of the things I want to show you, but don't be afraid to let go. Your sweet inhibition is all you have left when it comes to me and you.

Oh baby, make that phone call. I want to put your butt early to bed. Over and over, I tried to give you everything until I had no more to give. You'd always come to me and say, "Baby I need you more than anything, and I would always find ways to give you more, and I found myself falling apart, trying to please someone that I loved, and that I would love to hate because they were breaking my heart.

But, still, you'd come back on bending knees and begging me please, that there's no way you can live without me or can go on this way. Slowly, I had to find a way to let you go, because you were making me absolutely no good for myself or the next person that comes along and wants to be in my life.

NEVER

Never have I
loved you
more than
I do, right now.
I didn't mean
to cry,
I couldn't control
those tears.
They, like you,
just got away
from me.
I don't have
anymore
insanity pleas,
to get you
to stay.
I was holding
onto you
for dear life,
like my life
depended upon it.
Now, I am
going have to
pick myself up
and start
all over again.
The more I accept
this is part of life,
I will not die right here.

My Grandmother

As my grandmother would say, "Baby I can't tell you where it doesn't hurt. It hurts everywhere." No, she's not in a better place yet. She lives where two roads meet. At ninety three years old, and she's still threatening to slap folks, as soon as she gets up from her sit down position.

My grandmother always makes good on her promise. Most people are banking that she'd forget. But, just when you least expect, while you're trying to help her up; she's leaning forward to commence to spanking your backside.

I tell everyone, don't play with my grandmother. She has too much, "Get back in her." I love and celebrate having such a sweet grandmother; tells you in a second, "Don't play with me. I might be getting old, but that doesn't mean, I won't slap the mess out of you."

    I love you grandma' forever and ever!
       Now, she's in a better place
       R.I.P Mary Celestine Fowler

No More

No more heart, I have been trying to talk to you. It's like when my car wouldn't start.

I find myself yelling and cursing because you don't seem to be listening. I don't know what the problem is. It could be out of water oil or transmission fluid.

I just want us to get our lives started, and moving in the right direction. And, I don't know how to fix the problem or make this thing work.

ACTING A FOOL

You'll never get anywhere in life by acting a fool or being a simple mother fucker.

You have to have your act together and stop doing silly shyt, that you know pisses everyone else off.

Eventually, you're going to get put off by the people that love you the most. Think for a moment, we all get tired.

Make it easy on all of us and get your shyt together or the next time you find yourself in some stuff, nobody is going to come and bail your simple ass out.

Black History

Black History Month
but I celebrate being Black
everyday.
it's nothing to be ashamed of,
no reason to raise your fist
in solidarity with a glove on.
Nothing I have to refrain from
where I sit, pray, or send my kids
off to school.
I live in this country under a Constitution
with a different set of rules.
I know this country
has come a very long way
and still has a ways to go.
Slavery is not only when
you take someone's
freedom away
and you shackle them to plow your
fields with no pay.
And you do to them what you will
if it's in your heart, you hang them
or aim to kill them where they stand.
I try to understand the then and now,
and I pray that we can move past those
days and continue to create equality
amongst ourselves.
I don't think that I will ever forget
this part of America history.
Just pray that we don't enslave any race,
no matter what's their nationality.
God intended all of mankind to be free.

It's Not My Fault

It's not my fault
I don't always have to give
fuel to my thoughts.
the ink comes from
everything I see and think.

I call it a painter's view
my colors are not always
red, white, and blue.
I know from growing up
It's best to keep walking
when someone in a group
is gritting' on you.

I look at questions
like life,
needing a reply.
we have a responsibility
for those that can't
until we die.

Soldiers die every day
on the battlefield
and we still ask why?
When I don't get the answer
I am looking for,
I go hard in prayer
interceding
is sometimes too much
for me to bare.

Runner's Creed

I am a Runner, it's not my fault. However I was chosen, it wasn't by default. God whispered in my ear, "It's time to get up and let your trials begin." A comes when boys have to grow up and be men.

So, I got up and stumbled out the door the first few mornings, and I grumbled within because everything ached and my feet felt sore. Me, myself, and I know that running is not for everyone.

But, as I got over my self-doubt and increased my faith. I dedicate each step of the way at getting better and putting distance between doubt and faith each day.

Running now is what I do best, encouraging others by saying the first few steps are always the hardest. But after those first few steps, faith slams the door on self-doubt, and this is what running is all about.

I Did Not Have To

I did not have to run today. I had covered many of the days behind me with early starts, late starts, and false starts because I heard the sound of a shot from somewhere else in my head.

I made some good decisions, far less bad decisions and split decisions, but I'll let you be the judge.

I did what some would consider the unthinkable. I stopped to tie my shoes, they were too tight. I had to loosen them up but I still finished the run in good time.

Isn't this what it's all about, finishing the race, and not letting one day or another determine your final outcome? That just knowing that you can each day is half the battle.

But you have to keep on fighting, because if you stop, it transcends that you are no longer a runner, but merely a spectator.

The "N" Word

Do you realize what you just called me? You may have heard someone else say the same thing, and even in that same tone. But, I've never given you permission or shown you any submission, so it's best that you change up and leave that "N' word calling alone.

The nerve of some people thinking they can confront you in the same like manner as someone that knows you, doesn't that just blow you?

Anyone that feels like being a hero today, come to save the person that just thought they come at me that away.

I can't be everybody's mama' and teacher at the same damn time. Pray for me, and that I don't hear a ringside bell go off. But, I'm not anybody's nigga.

A Race Against The Old Me

A race against the old me, there's no doubt who would win. Today's Ralph would win. Yesterday's Ralph was incredibly fast, but he was never ambitious enough and he always slowed down or quit without giving his best.

Today's Ralph runs with more heart, and determination. Yesterday's Ralph ran 10-15 miles and got nothing out of it. Today's Ralph took a page from every previous experience to push himself even further.

One thing could be said about the young Ralph, if it wasn't for him, I wouldn't be the runner that I am today. I know that you have to stay focused, maintain balance in your life and quitting on yourself, and giving your haters something else to laugh about is no longer an option.

My Child

I kind of knew something that most people can't see. That I am going to need an umbrella today, and we're not even expecting rain.

When she comes running back home to me only because it wasn't as glamorous as she thought it would be.

I am going to need my boots because I know it's going to get deep. The stories she will tell me, to make it sound believable; "Lions, tigers, and bears, oh my," will be my response.

And then, she will say, "You are making fun of me." And I will remind her, I tried to warn you that outside these doors, life is rough. I said, "I will always be here for you, no matter how it works out." Besides, what are daddies for?

I NEED YOU

I need you
you are a habit
I can't quit
I wake up paranoid
looking for you
like someone stole
all my shyt
I love you
that's the truth
you are A benefit
of my youth
by any other name
you are my sunshine
I am helpless without you
but hopeful we will be together
I went to sleep last night
and woke up this morning
with your lips touching mines.
sometimes a dream
last a lifetime
I stop looking in the mirror
cause I don't like what I see.
someone that is fragile as me
I don't want to stand alone
my world has been built around you,
making me strong.
you know you can save me
from self-destruction
never leave me without a love note
and a set of instructions
"BABY YOU WILL BE OKAY
BUT YOU KNOW I CANT STAY."

YOU CAN'T

YOU CAN'T GO THROUGH THIS WORLD
AND NOT KNOW WHO YOUR FRIENDS ARE.
HAVEN'T YOU WANTED TO KNOW AND NOT
JUST GUESS WHO WERE YOUR RIDE OR
DIE?
YOU ARE THE BEST.
PEOPLE ARE SO WHACK.
YOU ALWAYS HAVE TO WATCH
YOUR BACK.
I AM ONE TRUE TO THE CODE
I WILL DO WHATEVER IT TAKES,
SHORT OF SELL MY SOUL.
IF I CAN SEE YOU
I WILL GET TO YOU.
IF I CAN HEAR YOU
I WILL BUST THROUGH
A BRICK WALL.
IF YOU DECIDE TO TAKE
A LEAP OF FAITH
I WILL HELP BREAK YOUR FALL.
I DONT HAVE ANY SECOND THOUGHTS
THERE IS NEVER ENOUGH TIME
I ALWAYS TREAT EVERYTHING
LIKE A TICKING BOMB.
I BELIEVE A BEST FRIEND IS SOMEONE
THAT WILL ALWAYS BE THERE TO RESCUE
YOU, BEFORE YOUR WORLD BLOWS UP,
JUST LIKE MY MOM.

UNLEASHED

Is the microphone on? This is a message to the young and old, mentally disturbed, physically challenged, sexually confused, politically incorrect and last but not least, to myself, poetry is defined and composed in and out of every element in the universe, and I can not reverse the last verse, which was unrehearsed, stay awake for the next line.

It never seizes to exist, and it recreates itself through time, in time, in our genetic genes, so it's revolutionized, and unparalyze, and it cannot be stabilized, like a cardiac patient, as it races and paces through time. So I, digress, knowing that this is not my best expression of poetry.

But there's still no reason why you and I can't continue to try to find a truer and deeper root to living, and then dying, while running unopposed, poetry and prose still lives and rebirths itself, over and over through time.

Before I drop the mic, life is a process, but you don't have to have every experience to know or realize, that there will be repercussion for your acts of mistrust, poor judgment or lack of understanding of the higher power of Jesus Christ Himself who will come down from heaven and judge both the living and dead in Christ.

So, if you haven't made that decisions, poetry that has been here since the being of time, I strongly urge you to get down on both knee, not moment later, and ask Him for forgiveness. Which He will lovingly do, and then ask to be saved in His name. That's poetry, receiving the word. And to become a living witness for God. As my father would often say, " It doesn't have to make sense, just do it." I'm turning the mic off now.

Mr. Window

You see just about everything
Up the street and
Down the other side of the street.
The rising and setting
of the sun each day.
You saw me
when I first came
home from the hospital.
My first day of school,
and my day of graduation.
You've watched me mourn, and
 look away like there's no tomorrow.
Mr. Window you've seen
me growing up laughing and
playing outside, and many times come
running inside crying.
Never once did I acknowledge you
being a part of my life, other
than describing my house.
I live in the house where it
always looks like someone is looking
out the door, with the six-pane window.
Everyone and everything has a story,
I know you Mr. Window, that you have your own.
Thank you for being there. I'm just sorry
I seldom took notice of your life.

Disappointed

My father would walk into the room within a minute, and say, "Stop everything you're doing, and look at the mess you've made. Did you put any thought into this project or consider what you need to do before you started?"

I said, "I thought, he said, "Son, you didn't think or you would not have created the mess you've made." I said, "Do you want me to finish?" "Son, the best thing you can do is go sit down and await further instruction, when I need you to help me finish, what I ask you to do."

I went to sit in the corner of the room, and I watched him collect himself as well as data from thin air, as though someone was sending it to him (not fair).

He'd go to the wall and pull a pencil from his pocket and start drawing a diagram of the room and then from there, he'd draw all the upgrades of what a project should of look like. Then he looked over at me and says, "Come over here, son. Do you think you can hand me a hammer?" Sure, dad.

The Little People

The little people see us kiss but we hardly ever speak. When we hold hands in public, it feels so uncomfortable, I don't think it was part of Gods plans.

Every time I look at her I am wondering what was I thinking? And she looks away from me as though I am their worst enemy.

Anyone can make a mistake, but we cannot keep making those same mistakes over and over again, by sleeping with someone that we have no real intentions of keeping them in our lives past the next day.

Many times we find ourselves tied to someone we never knew or loved, because of the birth of a child.

Now the child is looking and wondering WTF is going on. Always be careful who you have sex with and always consider the consequences.

Find that special someone, so you won't be mad at yourself at having to explain to your little one or little ones later, why mommy and daddy don't get along. Don't ever tell them they were a mistake when you and I know, God had no part in it.

No One Touches My Heart

In the world with so many people, no one touches me anymore. Not my heart, my soul, or my pillow at night. I almost feel invisible to the one person that I care about, as they sit beside me watching a 60" HD T.V., or on a private phone call as though I were in another room of the house.

Maybe, I do need to grab the car keys and go out for a long drive and think about making some changes in my life, So, I can feel that I am alive.

I am not looking for a lot of attention, I don't want to be a part of someone else's life, So, when people see us together they look at you all surprised like I was something or someone you failed to mention. I feel that the person in my life is suspect #1.

Suspect #1 is someone that you are not so sure about or possibly cannot be trusted. As I am driving away from the house, the relationship and the person I thought I cared about, whom has brought me to this point, I can hear my grandmother's voice in my ear, "There are too many windows and doors in a house to stay inside of something that's not working for you." And she has never lied.

I can't speak for anyone else and their situation, but for me, I have to make decisions for myself. But knowing that, I am not a doormat, someone's dishwasher, or royal butt kisser. And no one should stay in any mess like this, without complaints. Go to God, stay in prayer and worship on both knees, by saying," Lord give me the strength to get up and walk away."

Me Oh My

Have you ever been so emotional
that you were a wreck? Not enough
makeup could hide your breakup.

I can't take the pettiness and lying.
To name a few, I am not taking sloppy
seconds and in my own home, nor
will I feel like I am a guest.

So, it must not have been intended
for us to be together, not laughing.
Something must have gone terribly
wrong.

Was it when I ran out
for eggs and milk, or when you stayed a little
late at your job until eight? It really
does not matter. Life is what it is, on
a silver platter. You can either take it or leave it.

It's All About Me

It's not what you think, it's not what you say.
For me, it's not really about you, even though
you're the first one to jump in the way, every time
I move or have something to say.

I want to live my life to the fullest, a lily has its
season. It shares in the joys and pains of others
but still reaches its full potential before the
end of its lifetime.

I still have places to go, people to see, and as sad as
a cliché' as it may sound, I have mountains I must
climb.

So, this isn't about you, it's more about me.
The only part of this that becomes about you,
is when I look up and see you standing in my way.

Boogie Man

I am not your Boogie Man. I wish I could hold you until the sun comes up in the morning. But you are too busy fighting me off of you at night, or away from you in the daytime. I don't know what monster (s) that are still lurking around the corner or chasing after you.

And, if they reign from your childhood or started pursuing you somewhere along the way. But, you've got to be able to see, that I am not the one jumping out of your closet. And, I am trying to find a way to keep you safe in my arms.

I'M IN A STRUGGLE

I'm in a struggle,
so know that
you're not alone.

My money has been
funny for a long time

When I start to feel stressed
and depressed, I go outside and
take my shirt off, exclaiming
to the world, I have nothing else
to give; my struggle real.

My meal is a peanut butter or
grill cheese sandwich and that's
on a good day.

I try my best to avoid clouds in case they decide to burst, but when they do, I'm thinking things can't get any worse.

I can't call my brother, his situation is all
banged up, and all he has left is his truck. With
no phone, we can't keep in touch.

Yesterday a man died alone on the city street,
homeless and no next of kin to notify.

Yes, the struggle is real, no matter
who or where you are. But don't ever stop
praying over it.

MY DRUNKEN HEART

I never wanted it to be like this. That every time I opened my mouth, I was telling a different story. But I never thought the days of my life would begin and end the way that it has. And the only one thing that I take full responsibility for is that I didn't pray often or enough.

I can't imagine how many times God was trying to reach out to me and I was too focused on something else to give him the time of day. Faith is not only believing in God but also seeking him out early before your day begins or and ends. Ultimately, everything rests in his hands.

Like a madman or an excellent caregiver, I should have seen this coming from around the corner, or I should have been better prepared for when something does happen in my house.

Always the little things we overlook, like the absence of a bird that used to sing outside my bedroom window in the morning. The unsettledness of ending conversations with the spouse and children. And the increase of more baseline music being played louder and louder, drowning out any possible chance of closer affection in the car or in our home sweet home.

No more car seats, playpens, or baby strollers, the house is almost fully grown. Everyone is looking at each other in the eye, but no one is seeing things eye to eye.

And now the children want to fight each other, and bark back at the parents that gave them life. Who wouldn't be angry at this particular point? My thoughts were and screamed," everyone packs your stuff up and leaves with less than a thirty days notice," I don't care!

But common sense prevailed before I could say or do anything. I had to turn the music off and have everyone in the house come and sit down.

Once everyone had started talking, it was not difficult to realize that everyone's spirit over time had changed. Their thoughts, feelings and emotions were being expressed, I realized I had really lost connection with my own family.

On a different level, who's hand was rocking the cradle while was at work each day or reading my children bedtime stories while I was too busy doing other things? Who were my children's friends in the neighborhood or at school that influenced them the most? And why didn't I pray each day for God to keep their hearts and minds on Him? Because, the little that I was doing, I figured it was more than enough, but now I know better.

God always finds a way to break my sleep and show me my world. Especially, when I didn't make enough time Him and He has no other way. So, now I know where my family gets acting out in front of me from and disturbing me while I am asleep. Lord, I cannot thank you enough. I know I need a lot more prayer time in my life. Amen!

No Matter What It Looks Like

No matter what it looks like or what the label says.
Nothing in this world is shatterproof.
Nothing in this world is 100 proof.

I don't care what the Pastor or the label says. I had moments in my mind that I thought she was going to live forever.

Grown men do cry at the drop of a dime and in the dark when they lose someone they love and think that no one is looking. Life is like a game of chess, your next move is a challenge and always in your face. "How am I going to do this? Maybe I should suffer the consequences and do this."

Every now and then, I find myself calling myself taking a break, by refocusing my attention and doing other things. By doing other things or involving ourselves in other things, it creates a bigger distraction from making your next best move.

We know smoking, drinking and procreating takes away from your participation but the game of survival remains with us like chess pieces on the board.

Get your head back into the game, outside of God there are some things you have to control and put your required attention upon. To live, and be successful, you come to the realization that this game will continue with or without your involvement.

So your behavior of acting, being inattentive or ignorant does not excuse you. It will leave you as a possible victim of circumstance, being at the wrong place at the wrong time. Before someone says, "Your move" you should have already given it some thought.

The condition of life is to always think ahead, win, lose or draw. The game for you will eventually end but you don't have to tilt your queen. When you find love, find a way to keep this love together for as long as you live. In all your unresolved issues, always find peace.

God made us all unique, in his living divine spirit, but we've managed to ignore most of his teaching and go in a separate path, but let God be the judge and jury. We should always pray that our thoughts and decisions is with His influence and not the worlds. I know, it's my move.

HAVE YOU BEEN FAITHFUL?

HAVE YOU BEEN FAITHFUL?

- I have not

WHEN YOU SAW MY CHILDREN WITHOUT FOOD AND

CLOTHING, DID YOU TRY TO FEED THEM ALL?

-I did not

AS MANY HOMELESS PEOPLE IN THE WORLD, DID YOU

EVER OFFER ONE SHELTER FOR A NIGHT?

- I did not

WHEN THE ENTIRE WORLD WAS ASLEEP DID YOU PRAY

ONCE FOR THEM, WITHOUT INCLUDING YOUR OWN

PERSONAL REQUEST?

- I have not

Saying Goodbye

Today I have to say goodbye but I'd rather hear you laughing than to see you all cry. My life has been good but the past few years as I tried to do better to get better has been a rough ride. It has brought us closer together, and it was a great feeling to have family and friends that stuck by my side.

They tell you to enjoy your life knowing one day, you will leave to a better place. And so, I always tried to show kindness to everyone, and love those around me. I was never perfect, but I always took strides to be.

I want you to be better and do better and seek out your God given gifts and live out your dreams because life was given to each and every one of us to be enjoyed.

And if you don't have peace with someone, make peace with that someone. The heart can't hold the weight of anything other than love. If you thought I was going to leave out the most important part, I can't. God wants us to live each day in love, peace, and harmony; seeking out and finding our purpose in life.

And when you find your purpose and become that carpenter, keep building your faith each day in Jesus. The Lord will instruct you how to live and to be of good cheer I'm leaving now, but I only want to hear you laugh, and I don't want to see you cry. Let God be God in all your lives as I have lived.

Frank "The Barber"

I miss Frank
Frank was my Hair Barber;
He was our Barber.
No matter what time of day it was
or day of the week, Frank always greeted
me and everyone with a smile.
His day came too soon.
I didn't know the pain he carried.
I didn't see it on his back, and he
didn't wear on his face.
Every day Frank had a story to tell,
and every now and then, when
he'd lean a little closer to your ear,
you knew then his unpopular opinion
was for me and those sitting in close
proximity to hear.
I miss Frank,
and though I've moved on in other areas
of my life, but no other Barber have I
yet considered. Frank wasn't just another
Barber, he was my friend.
But, when I reflect on all the stories he's shared with
me, I remember him leaning in closer
and telling me in my ear, "I am going to be okay
because I know the Lord, and I've already
given my life to Jesus."

I miss Frank, but I know he's in a much better place, telling stories about life, the right and wrong roads he's taken, and how he ended up in prison. And whenever he gave advice about crime in the streets and drugs ruining our younger generation; that's how they got me.

He was speaking from his heart and personal experiences. I miss Frank, but I thank God for allowing this man of God to cut my hair. Really, his bottom line to every story, if you have the chance or get the chance, make things right. He wasn't just a Hair Barber but a fighter, helping everyone to win over life's situations, no matter what the day looks like and what the streets throw at you, keep your chin up.

LET ME BREAK THIS DOWN

Let me break this down to you. You cannot love everyone. Everyone is not your friend. You cannot live with everyone, no matter how good of a relationship you've had with them over the years. This is one of the best ways to ruin it.

If you're the child, act like an adult or grow-up. Only second to lending them money, please note you're not an institution. It's just best to help them find another affordable place to live, than to keep giving them the money.

It's a funny thing about trust, you cannot trust everyone. Let me say this again another way. You put your trust in God. Not in your brother, not in your sister, mother, father, or bestie for the past twenty years.

And we're not excluding any Pastors, get the picture? The statistics are alarmingly high of those that entrusted themselves to someone else with their lives or livelihood.

It appears that I have accomplished being quite negative, but my overall purpose is for you to build better relationships.

People have a way of destroying our lives from the insides out, no matter what their initial intentions were, with the spirits in this world we have to be careful. All things are subject to change, but they are not changing, when they want to know, "What's in your wallet?"

And, if a person is offended by you protecting yourself, shame on them. And pray God touches their heart.

THE GREATEST GIFT IS LOVE

In this crazy mixed up world sometimes, we need help from someone or something to come in and whisk us up and away. I have found myself struggling sometimes or caught up in a situation I can't fight my way out of or just make myself wake-up.

I have learned to go through the Drive-Thru in this world looking for an escape route, but after 2:36 p.m. on Riverside Drive on a Friday afternoon, there are none, you're stuck going nowhere.

I have found myself crying in church with unrelenting tears, and saying aloud, "God I need you, over and over again." After walking out those doors it seemed to have worked, but sometimes my faith isn't always there, and I slip and fall a lot faster and harder, and it truly hurts when I am not paying attention.

One day, when it mattered most, I found myself in a tight spot and I remembered a story my father had told me, about how he got hurt in battle, laying in the field on enemy territory, and he prayed.

Out of nowhere, a helicopter came down to the ground in the midst of the smoke and during the exchange of gunfire, it whisk him up and away. He said son if you ever need help just call on Jesus, and He will send you a helicopter, but you have to believe.

REAL FRIENDS

I woke up this morning crying about how much I miss my real friends. Now, I'm all grown up, with quote-unquote responsibilities; where the fun out of life is gone.

I go to work.

I go to church (nothing personal God)

I mow the lawn.

I volunteer all my extra time on my days off.

You need a Kodak camera to completely recapture this moment in time. Real friends call you up and ask you if you want to go get high?

Convince you by saying, "It'll make you feel better, to at least give it a try." With Real friends, you go out and party all night, and then hand you the car keys, and says "It's your turn to drive home."

Real friends go the distance with you, but off to the side, let you know that you were wrong; or we both were wrong for throwing rocks at the church window, sorry God again (nothing personal)

Real friends, you share your problems with, and not your Co-workers, not your next door neighbor and definitely not your Pastor; (nothing personal God.) I just don't need my business preached on Sunday. Friends are the ones that never seem to struggle to help you, especially when they see that you're in need.

Real friends are the best people in the world to have in your life, even if they don't have a nickel or dime bag of weed to share with them.

MY PARENTS WERE RIGHT

-My parents thought I'd never amount to anything. I didn't stay in the church, I hung out with the wrong crowd, sold drugs to earn a living, and all the while in the back of my mind I wanted to prove them wrong. I kept telling them, "I am going to be okay, besides there's not a Cop in this world that can catch me."

What I thought, I'd make a few quick dollars here and there, and then call it quits for good. Bad moments and great moments kept happening, one train after another. I would get caught and popped for some stupid stuff, serve a few short months, and be right back into my game tomorrow.

- It got to the point, my parents didn't want me to come over to the house, but in my mind, I haven't really, never grew up and that is the place I know as home.

I often find myself crashing into the curb or wall, right outside their front door. I make it up their front stairs, and I start screaming open up it's me! I know you are both in there.

- I know my dad would have let me in the last time, but my mom always struggled with him for the keys. I can always hear one them saying, "I love him too, but he has to learn sometimes, and we can't keep letting him in."

So, I would say, "McDonald's has a special, two for one, I got one and yours is free." If my little brother is anywhere in the house tonight, I would hear him laughing,

Ma', I just need to lay down for the night and I will be gone in the morning, besides I can't stop this bleeding and it won't stop on its own.

THE END-

www.ingramcontent.com/pod-product-compliance
Lightning Source LLC
Chambersburg PA
CBHW070206100426
42743CB00013B/3073